Mediterranean Bowls Cookbook

A Collection of 80 Healthy Greek, Spanish, Lebanese, and Italian Bowl Recipes (2022 Guide for Beginners)

Rita Curry

Table of Contents

Introduction

Mediterranean cuisine is famous since it is one of the healthiest on the planet. The advantages of these dishes make them even more appetising because they are prepared using fresh ingredients. Fresh foods such as berries, grains, herbs, vegetables, and nuts are emphasised in the diet.

Mediterranean cuisine refers to a wide range of eating patterns practised by a diverse group of people. It is unrelated to any particular ethnic group or community. Mediterranean cookery is influenced by a multitude of cultural variables.

The Mediterranean Sea was the birthplace of the world's first civilizations. Food land was aided by good soil and a temperate environment. Merchants selling cultural items like spices and delicacies were lured to their location at the crossroads of Europe, Asia, and Africa.

Another aspect that influenced Mediterranean food was colonisation. The many cultures of the Mediterranean came into closer contact as a result of multiple civilizations' endeavours to establish empires.

Olive oil is one of the most commonly used ingredients in Mediterranean cuisine. The area is highly wooded and densely planted with olive trees.

Olives play a significant role in a wide range of cuisines. Veggies are also necessary. Common vegetables include zucchini, green beans, carrots, tomatoes, nuts and seeds, mushrooms, garlic, okra, eggplants, and a variety of greens and courgettes. Meat is rarely consumed.

Because the rugged topography of the Mediterranean does not sustain larger herding animals such as cattle, goats, pigs, and poultry supply: most meat is generally roasted. Sheep and goat milk may also be used in several cuisines.

Seafood is widely accessible due to the city's proximity to the Mediterranean Sea. Mediterranean cuisine is defined by fresh herbs such as garlic, marjoram, tarragon, thyme, oregano, shallots, parsley, basil, and cloves.

The "Mediterranean Bowls Cookbook" has a plethora of tasty Mediterranean cuisine. Recipes are provided in Spanish, French, and Greek in the chapters. Begin by reading this book to learn about the health benefits of Mediterranean Bowls food.

Chapter 1
Recipes for Spanish Bowls

Grilled Chicken Rice Bowl

- ❖ **Cooking Time: 5 minutes**
- ❖ **Servings For 4**

Ingredients: Spanish rice

- 1 tsp lemon juice
- seasoned with salt & pepper
- a quarter teaspoon cumin
- 1 tsp tomatoes paste
- 1/4teaspoons dried oregano
- 1/2 tsp. paprika
- 5 ripe cherry tomatoes
- 1/8 cup coriander
- 1 tablespoon melted butter
- 1 garlic clove
- 1 cup of rice
- 2 c. water

Method:

1.   Melt the butter with the garlic in a skillet over medium heat.

2.   Simmer for thirty seconds, or until fragrant, before adding the tomatoes and continuing to cook.

3.   Cook the rice and parsley in the oil for 3 minutes.

4.   While the rice is heated in the pan, prepare another pot with tomato paste, cumin, water, oregano, lime juice, paprika, salt, and pepper.

5.   Reduce the heat to low and keep cooking.

6.   Arrange the grilled chicken slices and toppings on top.

Mexican Rainbow Rice Bowls

❖   **Time to cook:** 15 minutes
❖   **Servings For 4**

Ingredients: Vegetarian Mexican Rice Grilled veggies

- Mango
- Cilantro
- spiciness
- Lettuce Romaine
- Lime
- Beans (15 oz.)
- Tomato Salsa
- Avocado, sliced
- Red bell peppers
- Jalapeno
- a pinch of salt

Method:

1. Divide the rice into two dishes.
2. Add the seasoned beans and toss to combine.
3. Arrange your favourite toppings on top and serve!

Chicken Burrito Bowl

❖ **Cooking Time: 1 hour**
❖ **4 servings**

Ingredients:

- 1/4 cup stander
- 2 cups shredded cheddar cheese
- 2/3 cup corn
- a third cup of black beans
- 2 c. salsa
- 2 teaspoon seasoning blend
- Kosher salt with black pepper
- 4 servings brown rice
- a single lime
- 2 breasts of chicken
- 1/2 cup diced red onion

Method

1.   In a small dish, combine onions and fresh lemon juice from 2 lemon slices.
2.   Pat the chicken breasts dry.
3.   Grill on an oiled grill pan over medium-high heat.
4.   Remove the chicken from the fire and let the outside for at least five minutes before slicing it.
5.   In a large mixing bowl, combine cooked black beans, cilantro, rice, taco spices, salsa, corn onion/lime mixture, and chicken.
6.   Cook on medium-high to completely heat.
7.   Garnish with a dusting of cheese.

Fajita Bowls with Mushrooms

❖   **Time to cook: 30 minutes**
❖   **Servings For 2**

Ingredients:

- 2 teaspoons olive oil
- 1/4 oz. cilantro, salt
- 3 tbsp. soured cream
- 1 onion, red
- a single jalapeno peeled
- 2 tablespoons chimichurri mixture
- Spanish rice, 7 oz.
- 3 cloves garlic
- a single lime
- Cremini mushrooms, 8 oz.

Method

1.	Preheat the oven to 375 degrees Fahrenheit.
2.	Combine the lime juice, red onion, chimichurri sauce, garlic, olive oil, cremini mushrooms, and salt in a large mixing bowl.
3.	Toss everything together and leave aside for 10 minutes to marinate.
4.	Arrange the marinated mushrooms and onions on a baking sheet.
5.	Roast until the mushrooms are tender and the onions are gencaramel of sitefor about 20 minutes.
6.	Bring a small pot halfway full of water to a boil.
7.	Turn off the heat, add the Spanish rice, cover, and leave aside for eight minutes.
8.	In a medium mixing bowl, combine the mango slaw, remaining mango, red onion, and sliced jalapeño.
9.	Serve mushroom fajitas with sour cream and cilantro leaves and stems on top.

Fiesta Bowl (Mexican Rice)

❖ **Time to cook: 30 minutes**
❖ **Servings For 5**

Ingredients:

- Avocado organic Black beans organic
- Mexican cheese mix
- Caritas
- Roasted corn, frozen
- 2 tbsp chicken broth
- 1 tin of tomato sauce
- 1teaspoons of sea salt
- 4 garlic cloves
- 2 c. jasmine rice
- a quarter teaspoon cumin
- 1/2 sour onion
- 2 teaspoons melted butter

Method:

1. In a large heavy-bottomed pan or Dutch oven, heat the oil until it sparkles.
2. Cook for 2 minutes, or until the onion has softened.
3. Toss in the rice to cover all of the grains with oil.
4. Continue to stir often until the rice begins to brown.
5. Cook for 1 minute, or until the salt, cumin, and garlic are aromatic.
6. Bring the broth and tomato sauce to a boil.
7. Cook, covered, for about 15 minutes, or until all liquid has been absorbed.

Taco Bowls with Ground Turkey

❖ **Time to cook: 15 minutes**
❖ **Servings For 4**

Ingredients: the Turkey Tacos

- 1/4 cup apple cider vinegar 2 tbsp avocado oil
- 1 teaspoon chipotle powder 1/2cups chicken broth
- three tbsp tomato paste
- 1 teaspoon dried oregano
- 1 teaspoon paprika, 1 teaspoon salt
- 2 teaspoons minced garlic
- 3 tablespoons cumin
- 2 tsp coriander (cilantro)
- 1/3 cup sliced white onion
- 1 teaspoon chilli powder
- 1.5   pound

turkey for Cauliflower Rice
- 1/2 cup chicken broth (about)
- cilantro, fresh
- 1 teaspoon sea salt
- two tbsp tomato paste
- 3 garlic cloves
- 1 tablespoon cumin
- 1 teaspoon olive oil
- 1/2 cup onions
- 1 huge head of cauliflower

Method:

1.   Heat a large pan over medium heat and preheat the oven to 350°F.

2.	Once the pan is hot, add the onion and oil.

3.	Allow for another 2-3 minutes of boiling before adding the ground turkey or beef.

4.	Continue stirring to achieve even cooking of the meat.

5.	Season the meat with spices.

6.	In a mixing bowl, combine the apple cider vinegar, tomato paste, and vegetable broth.

7.	Allow for 3-5 minutes of cooking time.

8.	Melt the butter in a large pan over medium-high heat.

9.	Sauté the onion for 3 minutes.

10.	In a mixing dish, combine the salt, cauliflower rice, and cumin.

11.	Gently toss the vegetable mixture to coat it.

12.	Turn the heat up to medium-high and add the tomato paste, followed by 1/4by broth.

13.	Layer the cauliflower rice on the bottom, then top with taco meat.

Zucchini Spanish Rice Burrito Bowls

❖	**Time to cook: 45 minutes**
❖	**Servings For 6**

Ingredients: Spanish Rice with Zucchini

- 1 zucchini (medium)
- 1 cup grated cheddar
- 1 cup chicken stock
- 1 quart s1-quart tsp chilli powder
- 1/4 tsp smoked paprika

- 1 cup rice, uncooked
- a quarter teaspoon cumin
- 3 tbsp of yellow onion
- 2 garlic cloves
- 1 teaspoon olive oil

Mushrooms and chicken

- 1/2 tsp seasoned salt
- 8 ounces mushrooms
- 1/2 tsp cumin 1/2 tsp garlic powder
- 1 tablespoonchilli
- 1/2 teaspoons dried oregano
- 22-ppoundchchicken breast teaspoons olive oil

Method

1.   Heat the olive oil in a large saucepan over medium heat for one minute.
2.   After adding the onion, cook for 3 minutes.
3.   Stir in the rice and spices and continue to boil.
4.   Bring the chicken stock and salsa to a boil.
5.   Prepare both the chicken and the mushrooms.
6.   Season the chicken with cumin, garlic powder chilli powder, oregano, and salt.
7.   Brown the seasoned chicken over medium-high heat.
1.   Cook for 8 minutes in the same skillet as the chopped mushrooms.
8.   Cover the skillet and leave it off the heat for 5 minutes, or until the cheese has melted and the zucchini is tender.

Bowl of Spanish Rice and Beans

❖   **Time to cook: 50 minutes**
❖   **Servings per recipe: 6**

Ingredients:

- 3 cups veggie broth
- Green olives, 1/3 cup
- 1 tomato can
- kidney beans, 2 cans
- 1/4 tsp cayenne pepper
- 2 cups uncooked white rice
- 1 teaspoon dried oregano
- 1/2 tsp black pepper
- 1 tablespoon kosher salt
- 1 tablespoon chilli powder
- 3 cloves garlic
- 1 tsp paprika
- 1 onion, yellow
- 2 teaspoons olive oil

Oil of Parsley

- 3 tbsp olive oil 1/2 tsp lemon zest
- 3 tbsp parsley (leaves)

Method:

1. Heat the oil in a large skillet with a tight-fitting lid over medium heat.
2. Cook, stirring occasionally, for 5 minutes, or until the onion is softened.
3. Cook for 60 seconds, stirring often, until the oregano, garlic, salt, black pepper, chilli powder, paprika, and cayenne pepper are aromatic.
4. Cook for 2 minutes, or until the rice is translucent.
5. In a mixing dish, combine the beans, tomatoes, and broth.
6. Bring the mixture to a boil, then reduce to low heat and simmer for around 30 minutes.
7. Meanwhile, create parsley oil in a separate bowl by whisking together lemon zest, parsley, lemon juice, and olive oil.

Chapter 2
Recipes for Italian Bowls

Italian Power Pasta Bowl

❖ **Cooking Time: 40 minutes**
❖ **Size of each serving: 16**

Ingredients:

- 11-quartpesto sauce
- 3 quarts alfredo sauce
- 4 penne pasta, 1/2 oz.
- 4 quarts marinara sauce
- 60 little shrimp
- 5 breasts of chicken

Method:

1.	Put together a meal using noodles and a variety of toppings.
2.	Combine your favourite sauce with the prepared components!

Meatball Italian Bowl

- ❖ **Cooking Time 30 minutes**
- ❖ **Size of each serving: 4**

Ingredients:

- 24 oz. marinara sauce
- The parmesan cheese
- Meatballs, 1/2 oz.
- 1 broccoli head
- 1 pound penne pasta

Method

1. Distribute the ingredients evenly among the four bowls.
2. To roast your broccoli, clean it, chop it, and sprinkle it in olive oil.
3. Season with salt and pepper to taste.
4. Bake for 5-10 minutes at 375°F on a baking sheet until soft.
5. Cook the pasta according to the package directions.
6. Cook the meatballs until done.
7. Place the pasta in a mixing basin.
8. Place the meatballs in a mixing bowl.
9. Add the roasted broccoli to the mixing bowl and toss to combine.
10. Add the marinara sauce.

Bowls of Italian Minestrone

❖ **Time to cook: 50 minutes**
❖ **Servings per recipe: 6**

Ingredients:

- 1 vegetable mixture
- 1 cannellini bean (cannellini)
- 1 teaspoon minced garlic
- 2 cups chicken broth
- 1/2 lb. chicken breast
- 1 teaspoon of seasoning
- 1 tablespoon melted butter
- 8 oz. spaghetti

Method:

1. Cook the pasta according to the package directions.
2. In the meantime, in a 4-quart pot, melt the butter and add the chicken, herb seasoning, and garlic.
3. Cook, stirring occasionally, on medium-high heat.
4. In a large mixing bowl, combine the vegetables, broth, and beans.
5. Continue to cook for another 8-10 minutes, stirring occasionally.
6. Remove from the heat and set aside to cool for 15 minutes.
7. To serve, divide the spaghetti evenly among six individual dishes and top with the chicken mixture.

Bowl of Italian Polenta

❖ **Time to cook: 30 minutes**
❖ **Servings per recipe: 6**

Ingredients:

- Toppings
- roasted red peppers in a jar
- The parmesan cheese
- Hearts of artichoke
- Green or black olives
- Meatballs
- Onions, red

Polenta

- 1/2 tsp kosher salt
- 1/2teaspoons black pepper
- 1/4cups grated parmesan cheese
- ricotta cheese, 1/3 cup
- 1/2cups cooked polenta
- 1/4 cup tomato
- 3 garlic cloves
- 4 cups chicken stock
- 2 tsp. Italian seasoning
- 1 teaspoon olive oil

Method:

1. Prepare the meatballs or sausage according to package directions.
2. Preheat a medium-sized saucepan over low heat.
3. Add the olive oil.

4.   In a mixing bowl, combine the Italian seasoning and red pepper flakes.
5.   After adding the garlic, sauté for 30 seconds.
6.   Fill the pot halfway with chicken broth.
7.   After slowly whisking in the polenta, cook for 3 to 5 minutes.
8.   After the polenta has hardened, add the ricotta cheese, sun-dried tomatoes, Parmesan cheese, salt, and pepper.
9.   Garnish with cooked meatballs or sausage.

Bowls of Italian bread

❖   **Time to cook: 1 hour 75 minutes**
❖   **8 servings**

Ingredients:

- 1 beaten egg white
- 1 teaspoon water
- 7 cups AP flour
- 1 teaspoon cornmeal
- a teaspoon of salt
- 2 teaspoons olive oil
- 1/2 cup warm water
- 2 (1.25 oz.) packages dry yeast

Method:

1.   In a large mixing bowl, dissolve the yeast in warm water.
2.   Set aside for 10 minutes to allow the mixture to become creamy.
3.   Combine the yeast mixture, oil, salt, and 5 cups flour in a large mixing bowl and thoroughly combine.
4.   Stir in the remaining flour 1/2 cup at a time.
5.   Shape each portion into a 4-inch round loaf.
1.   Preheat the oven to 400 degrees F.
6.   Combine the egg white and one tablespoon of water in a mixing bowl; lightly rub half of the egg wash over the loaves.
7.   Bake in a preheated oven for 15 minutes.
8.   Brush the top with the remaining egg mixture and bake for another 5 to 10 minutes, or until golden.

Meal Prep Bowls with Italian Chicken

- ❖ **1 hour cooking time**
- ❖ 4 servings

Ingredients:

- 2 tablespoons olive oil
- 4 to 6 cups cooked rice
- 1 zucchini (medium)
- 2 teaspoons minced garlic
- 1 red onion, small
- 1 plum tomato cup
- Chicken breasts weighing 0.91 kg
- 1 pound broccoli florets
- 2 teaspoons fresh thyme
- 1 teaspoon paprika
- 2 teaspoons marjoram
- 2 teaspoons rosemary
- ½ teaspoon pepper
- 2 teaspoons basil
- 1 teaspoon sea salt

Method:

1.	Preheat the oven to 232 degrees Fahrenheit.
2.	Combine thyme, rosemary, salt, marjoram, basil, pepper, and paprika in a small bowl.
3.	In a baking dish, combine the chicken and vegetables.
4.	Scatter all the seasonings and garlic evenly over the meat and vegetables.
5.	Sprinkle with olive oil.
6.	Bake for 15-twenty minutes, or until meat is cooked and vegetables have charred slightly.
7.	On top of the rice, evenly distribute the chicken and vegetables.
8.	Cover and keep in the fridge for 2- 5 days or serve for supper!

Italian Meatball Quinoa Bowls

❖ **Cooking Time: 20 minutes**
❖ **4 servings**

Ingredients

- 1 jar marinara sauce
- 2 cups cooked quinoa
- 1 cup breadcrumbs
- ½ cup water
- ½ cup grated Parmigiano
- ¼ cup Italian parsley
- 1 ½ pounds ground beef
- 2 large eggs
- 2 cloves garlic
- Pinch red pepper
- 1 large onion
- Salt, to taste
- Extra-virgin olive oil

Method

1.   In a big pan, heat the olive oil.
2.   Combine the salt, onion, and garlic in a mixing bowl.
3.   Cook until the onions are very tender and browning.
4.   Remove from the oven and set aside to cool.
5.   Combine the onion combination, red pepper, ground beef, breadcrumbs, eggs, parsley, Parmigiano-Reggiano, and water in a large mixing bowl.
6.   Form the meat mixture into balls of the appropriate size.
7.   In the same pan, heat some more olive oil.
8.   Cook for 15 minutes over medium heat or until browned on both sides.
9.   Cook for another 5 minutes after adding the marinara sauce.

Italian Sausage and Broccoli Bowls

❖ **Time to cook: 30 minutes**
❖ **Size of each serving: 4**

Ingredients:

- 2 cups grains
- 4 oz. mozzarella cheese
- 1 teaspoon sugar
- 4 Italian sausages
- 2 pints grape tomatoes
- 2 garlic cloves
- 1 teaspoon olive oil
- seasoned with salt & pepper
- 1 bunch broccoli

Method:

1. Preheat the oven to 475 degrees Fahrenheit.
2. Chop one bunch of broccoli to florets, put them out on a large baking sheet.
3. Roast until browned, toss with kosher salt, olive oil, and pepper.
4. Cook three to four Italian sausages in a nonstick pan over medium heat.
5. In a pan, combine 2 quarts of grape tomatoes, two peeled and crushed cloves of garlic and sugar.
6. Cook on a medium-high heat setting.
7. Slice the sausages and serve with broccoli.

Chapter 3
Mediterranean Bowls Recipes

MediterraneanBulgur Bowl

- ❖ **Cooking Time: 30 minutes**
- ❖ **4 servings**

Ingredients:

- 2 tablespoons fresh mint
- 2 tablespoons lemon juice
- ½ cup feta cheese ¼ cup hummus
- 2 cups cherry tomatoes
- 1 red onion, small
- 1 can garbanzo beans
- 6 ounces baby spinach
- 1 cup bulgur
- ¼ teaspoon salt
- 2 c. water
- a quarter teaspoon cumin

Method

1.   Combine the first four ingredients in a stockpot and bring to a boil.
2.   Reduce heat to low and cook, covered, for 10-1/2 minutes, or until vegetables are soft.
3.   Heat through the garbanzo beans.
4.   Remove from the fire and add the spinach.
5.   Allow it to sit for a few minutes, covered until the spinach has wilted.
6.   Combine the remaining ingredients in a mixing bowl.

Mediterranean Tilapia Power Bowls

- ❖ **Time to cook: 45 minutes**
- ❖ **Size of each serving: 4**

Ingredients:
Tilapia Fillets

- ½ teaspoon red pepper flakes
- ½ teaspoon cumin powder
- 1/2 teaspoon black pepper
- 1 tablespoon oregano leaves
- Juice from ½ lemon
- 1 teaspoon sea salt
- 4 garlic cloves
- 3 tablespoons olive oil
- 4 Tilapia fillets

Lemon Herb Tahini Dressing

- 6 tablespoons cold water
- 1 teaspoon ground cumin
- Juice from a lemon
- 2 teaspoon salt
- ½ cup tahini paste

Greek Power Bowls

- 1 cup pickled red onions
- Pita bread for serving
- 2 cups chickpeas
- 1 cup feta cheese
- 2 cups cherry tomatoes
- 2 cups cucumbers
- 2 cups quinoa

Method:

1. Whisk the lime juice, tahini paste, cold water, salt, and powdered cumin in a small bowl.
2. Season with more salt or spices.
3. Whisk together the garlic cloves, sunflower oil, and other spices in a small bowl.
4. Marinate the Tilapia fillets in the marinade.
5. Refrigerate for half an hour after covering.
6. Cook for 2–3 minutes on each side in a grill pan or large skillet with a sprinkle of olive oil.
7. Drizzle lemon herb tahini dressing over each bowl of marinated Tilapia fillets

Mediterranean Buddha Bowl

- ❖ **1 hour to prepare**
- ❖ **Size of each serving: 4**

Ingredients:

- 1 cup sliced red onion
- Chickpeas (15 oz.)
- 4 ounces quinoa
- a cup of cucumber
- 1 teaspoon lemon
- 1 tsp za'atar seasoning
- 1 tsp. garlic powder
- 1 teaspoon tahini
- four tbsp olive oil
- 4 cups of kale
- 1 large eggplant

Method:

1. Preheat the oven to 425 degrees F.
2. In a separate baking dish, combine the oil, greens, and garlic powder.
3. Place the kale and eggplant in the oven after fully mixing.
4. Roast the kale and eggplant until well browned and done.
5. In a separate dish, combine the remaining olive oil, lime juice, tahini, and za'atar.
6. To assemble the Buddha bowls, divide the grains among four bowls, top with roasted kale, peel the eggplant, and divide the bowls.

Mediterranean Hummus Bowl

❖ **Cooking Time: 40 minutes**
❖ **Size of each serving: 4**

Ingredients: To make the Hummus

- 2-3 tbsp cold water
- salt, pepper
- 1/2 teaspoon cumin powder
- 1/2 teaspoon of salt
- 2 teaspoons olive oil
- 1/4 cup lemon juice
- 1-2 garlic cloves
- 1/4 tbsp tahini
- Chicchickpeas.8 oz.

Regarding the Bowl

- a few black olives
- A few fried pimientos
- 1/2 cucumbers
- ounces feta cheese
- Small tomatoes, 9 oz.
- 1 red onion, tiny
- 1/4 cup water
- Baby spinach leaves (1.8 oz.)
- Extra virgin olive oil
- Quinoa, 5.3 oz.
- 1/2 tsp onion powder
- 1/4 tsp paprika powder
- 1/2 tsp garlic powder
- 1 chickpea can

Method

1.   Combine the tahini and lime juice in a food processor and pulse for one minute.
2.   Combine the spice, olive oil, garlic, and salt in a mixing bowl until smooth.
3.   Add half of the chickpeas to the food processor/mixer and pulse for a few seconds longer, or until creamy.
4.   Stir in the remaining chickpeas and spices for another 1-2 minutes to make a smooth paste.
5.   Preheat the oven to 390 degrees F.
6.   Roast the chickpeas for 20-25 minutes, or until they are thoroughly browned.
7.   While the chickpeas roast, cook the quinoa according to per package directions.
8.   To prepare the dressing, whisk together some olive oil and fresh lemon juice, then season with salt and pepper to taste.

Mediterranean Chickpea Salad Bowl

❖   **Cooking Time: 10 minutes**
❖   **Size of each serving: 4**

Ingredients: Dressing

- 1/2 teaspoon agave syrup
- Season with salt to taste
- 2 tbsp vinegar (red wine)
- 1/2 tsp dried oregano
- 2 teaspoons lemon juice
- three tbsp olive oil
- 2 cloves garlic

Salad with Chickpeas from the Mediterranean

- 1/4 cup feta crumbled 1/3 cup red onion
- 1 cup sliced cherry tomatoes
- a quarter cup parsley leaves
- 1 pound cucumbers
- Chickpeas, 15.5 oz.

Regarding the Bowl

- 1 hummus with garlic
- 1 pita bread, warm
- arugula, 1/2 cup
- 1/2 cup cooked quinoa

Method:

1. In a large mixing basin, combine chickpeas, parsley, cucumbers, tomatoes, onion, and feta.
2. In a small container, mix the oregano, minced garlic, agave, olive oil, lemon juice, red wine vinegar, and salt to prepare the dressing.
3. Combine the salad and the dressing in a large mixing bowl.

Power Bowls with Red Pepper Sauce from the Mediterranean

❖ **Time to cook: 30 minutes**
❖ **Size of each serving: 4**

Ingredients:

- feta cheese, 3 oz.
- Lemon wedges and fresh basil
- 1/4 teaspoon black pepper 2 teaspoons rice vinegar
- a single avocado
- 1/2 cup sliced red onion
- 1/2 teaspoon cumin powder
- 1/2 cucumbers, English
- 1/2 tsp kosher salt
- 1 can chickpeas (15 oz.)
- 1 cup quinoa, dry

Sauce with Red Peppers

- 1/4 tsp red pepper flakes
- 1/4 tsp kosher salt
- 1 clove garlic
- 1 tablespoon paprika
- 1/4 cup extra virgin olive oil
- 1 jarred pepper (1/2 oz.)

Method:

1. Combine the water, quinoa, and salt in a skillet.
2. Bring to a boil, then reduce to low heat, cover, and leave to simmer for 15 to 20 minutes.

3.   Remove from the fire, add the chickpeas and cumin, and keep aside until ready to serve.
4.   While the quinoa is cooking, make the avocado-cucumber salad by combining vinegar, cucumber, red onion, avocado, remaining salt, and black pepper in a mixing bowl.
5.   Combine all of the ingredients for the red pepper sauce in a blender.
6.   Divide the quinoa and chickpea mixture among four dishes evenly.

Mediterranean Steak and Quinoa Bowl

❖   **1 hour cooking time**
❖   **4 servings**

Ingredients: Marinade

- 1/4 tsp of salt
- 2 tsp. Greek seasoning
- 1/2 tsp Dijon mustard 1/4 tsp honey
- 2 1/2tbsp. olive oil
- 2 1/2 tbsp red wine vinegar

Bowl

- 2/3 cup tomato
- a 1/2 cup cucumber
- 16 cups fresh baby spinach
- 3 quinoa cups

Tzatziki Sauce

- 1 pound sirloin steak
- 1/4 teaspoon black pepper 1/8 teaspoon kosher salt
- 1/2 tsp olive oil
- 1 tablespoon dried dill weed
- 1 teaspoon lemon juice
- 1/4 cup cucumber 1 teaspoon lemon zest
- 1/2 cup plain Greek yoghurt

Method:

1. Combine the marinade ingredients in a small bowl.
2. Place half of the marinade in a zip-top plastic bag, and keep the other half for basting.
3. Toss the meat with the Greek seasoning in the bag.
4. Marinate the sirloin for 15 minutes to 2 hours.
5. Preheat a grill pan on the stove over "MEDIUM-HIGH" heat.
6. Cook the steak for 10-1/2 minutes for medium-rare on a hot grill pan.
7. In a saucepan, steam the spinach while cooking the quinoa according to package recommendations.
8. Combine all of the Tzatziki sauce ingredients in a mixing basin.
9. The bowls are topped with tzatziki sauce and feta cheese.

Bowls of Mediterranean Cauliflower Rice Tabbouleh

❖ **Time to cook: 40 minutes**
❖ **4 servings**

Ingredients:

- 1/4 cup hemp hearts 1 cup hummus
- 1/2 ripe green olives
- 1 artichoke heart jar
- four green onions
- 1 (16-ounce) package tofu
- 1/2 cup fresh parsley
- 1 cup coriander
- Himalayan pink salt
- Pinch of black pepper
- 1 medium head of cauliflower
- 2 quarts tomatoes
- 1 lemon's juice
- 1 little red bell pepper

Method:

1.	Preheat the oven to 400 degrees F.
2.	In a food processor, pulse the cauliflower.
3.	Combine the grape tomatoes, red bell pepper, parsley and green onion, cilantro, and lemon juice in a large mixing dish.
4.	To mix the tastes, add a pinch of Himalayan sea salt and black pepper.
5.	In the meantime, prepare your herbed tofu.

6. Bake for 10–15 minutes, or until the veggies are tender.

7. To assemble the bowls, divide the cauliflower rice and herbed baked tofu among the bowls, then garnish with fresh parsley.

Bowls of Mediterranean Lentil and Grain

❖ **1 hour cooking time**
❖ **4 servings**

Ingredients:

- 1/2 tsp red pepper flakes
- 1/2 tsp whole peppercorns
- 1 teaspoon maple syrup
- 1/2 teaspoon coarse sea salt
- 3/4 cups of water
- 1/2 CUP APPLE CUCUMBER VINEGAR
- 1 onion, red

Farro

- black pepper, freshly cracked
- 2 cloves garlic
- salt kosher
- two bay leaves
- 2 1/2 cup water
- 1 quart (180g) farro
- Lentils with Creamy Mediterranean Flavors
- 2 teaspoons tahini
- 3 tamari teaspoons
- salt kosher
- to taste, black pepper
- 1 cup green lentils 2 23 cup vegetable broth
- 1 tablespoon cumin seeds
- 6 cloves garlic
- 1 teaspoon olive oil

Hummus a la mode

- black pepper
- freshly cracked
- 6 tbsp of cold water
- 1 tablespoon cumin
- 1 tsp. kosher salt
- 1 lemon, medium
- 2 cloves garlic
- 1 tbsp tahini
- 1 can chickpeas (15 oz.)

Method:

1.   In a large mixing bowl, combine the salt, hot water, red pepper flakes, maple syrup, vinegar, and peppercorns.
2.   Continue stirring until the sugar is completely dissolved.
3.   Heat the olive oil in a large saucepan over medium heat.
4.   Continue to cook until the garlic and cumin seeds are fragrant.
5.   Next, add the lentils and vegetable broth.
6.   Remove from the heat and whisk in the tahini and tamari until thoroughly mixed.
7.   Place the water in a medium saucepan, season with salt, and bring to a boil.
8.   In a mixing bowl, combine the faro and seasonings.
9.   In a food processor, combine the chickpeas for 2 to 3 minutes.
10.   In a mixing bowl, combine the garlic, tahini, cumin, lemon juice, and salt.
11.   Half-fill a serving plate with hummus.

Mediterranean Salmon Bowl

❖ **Cooking Time: 25 minutes**
❖ **Size of each serving: 4**

Ingredients: Regarding the Salmon

- 1/2 teaspoon of salt
- 1/8 teaspoon black pepper
- 1 tangerine
- 2 tsp. dried dill
- three tbsp olive oil
- Salmon (16 oz.)

Regarding the Bowls

- 1 teaspoon of seasoning
- 1/4 cup olive oil 2 garlic cloves
- 1 tangerine
- 5 spring onions
- 1/4 cup parsley, fresh
- 1 pound Kalamata olives
- 1/2 cucumbers, English
- 1 pound feta cheese
- 1/4 cup roasted red peppers
- 1 pound tomatoes
- 1 pound, 5 ounces lettuce

Method

1. Preheat the oven to 400 degrees Fahrenheit.
2. Arrange the fish on a baking pan and put it away.
3. Bake the fish in the oven for 15-20 minutes.
4. Take the salmon out of the oven and arrange it on a serving plate, flaking it into large bits.
5. Divide the ingredients among four dishes.
6. Arrange the salmon pieces in each dish.

Mediterranean Quinoa Salad Bowls

❖ **Time to cook: 15 minutes**
❖ **2 servings**

Ingredients:

- 1/4 cup kalamata olives 1/4 cup feta
- a 1/2 cup cucumber
- 1/4 cup sliced red onion
- 1/4 cup tomatoes 1/2 cup chickpeas
- 2 c. arugula
- 1/2 cup quinoa, dry

Dressing with Tahini

- 1/4 tsp. dill 1/4 tsp. oregano
- 18 teasteaspoonsck pepper
- 1/4 tsp garlic powder
- 1/2 tbsp apple cider vinegar
- 18teaspoonsn of salt
- 1 teaspoon olive oil
- 1 tbsp. balsamic vinegar
- three tbsp lemon juice
- 1 teaspoon tahini

Method:

1.   Cook the quinoa according to the package recommendations.
2.   Combine all of the ingredients in each bowl, including the sun-dried tomatoes, quinoa, and crumbled feta cheese.
3.   Combine all of the dressing ingredients in a small container.
4.   Shake the jar vigorously with the lid on until everything is well combined.

Mediterranean Avocado Salad

❖ **Time to cook: 25 minutes**
❖ **Size of each serving: 4**

Ingredients:

- 1/4 cup black olives 1/4 cups red onion
- 2 cups of tomatoes
- 1 cup feta cheese
- a cup of cucumber
- cups fresh parsley
- chickpeas, 2 cup
- bulger (four cups)

Hummus with Avocado

- 2 cloves garlic
- seasoned with salt & pepper
- 3 tablespoons avocado oil
- a teaspoon of lemon juice
- a single avocado
- a 1/2 cup of chickpeas

Vinaigrette with Lemon

- 1 tablespoon Dijon mustard
- Season with salt and pepper to taste.
- 2 tablespoons avocado oil
- 1/4 cup lemon juice (about)

Method

1.   In a blender, combine avocado, chickpeas, lemon juice, avocado oil, and finely sliced garlic.
2.   Blend until smooth, then season to taste with salt and pepper.
3.   In a medium mixing bowl, combine Dijon mustard, lemon juice, avocado oil, and salt and pepper to taste.
4.   Continue to stir until everything is well combined.
5.   Divide the ingredients evenly among large mixing basins.

Quinoa Bowls with Roasted Chickpeas from the Mediterranean

- ❖   **Time to cook: 30 minutes**
- ❖   **Size of each serving: 4**

Ingredients: Regarding Bowls

- 1/2 teaspoon of salt
- 4 cups salad greens, baby
- four tbsp parsley
- 1 lemon juice
- 1 pound tomatoes
- 1/4 onion, red
- 1 pound English cucumber
- To make Roasted Chickpeas
- 1/4 tsp of salt
- 1 tablespoon of olive oil

- 1/4 tsp turmeric 1/4 tsp garlic powder
- 1 tablespoon cumin
- 1/2 teaspoon dried oregano
- 1 chickpea can
- To make the Citrus Tahini Sauce, combine all of the ingredients in a mixing bowl.
- 1/2 tsp kosher salt
- 1/4 tsp black pepper
- 2 teaspoons lemon juice
- 1 garlic clove
- 3/4cupsp water
- 1 tbsp tahini

Regarding Quinoa

- 1 pound vegetable broth
- Black pepper with salt
- 1 cup quinoa, dry
- 1 teaspoon olive oil

Method:

1. Preheat the oven to 400 degrees F.
2. Toss the spices, chickpeas, and olive oil in a mixing dish.
3. Arrange them in an even layer on the prepared baking sheet.
4. Roast for 15 minutes, then add the chickpeas and roast for another 5 to 10 minutes.
5. Sauté the quinoa for two to three minutes.
6. Season to taste with salt and pepper.
7. To make the sauce, combine all of the ingredients in the bowl of a food processor or blender.
8. Process indefinitely until everything is well combined.

Bowls of Mediterranean Meatballs

- ❖ **Time to cook: 50 minutes**
- ❖ **2 servings**

Ingredients:

- 1 cup farro, uncooked
- 1/4 c. feta cheese
- Chickpeas, canned
- 1 cup sliced cherry tomatoes
- a 1/2 cup hummus
- 4 cups fresh baby spinach
- 1 medium cucumber
- smoked paprika, 1 tsp
- Add a pinch of salt and black pepper to taste.
- 2 tbsp. fresh dill
- 1 tablespoon vinegar (red wine)
- 1/3 cup onions
- 1 tbsp dried oregano
- 1 pound ground beef
- 2 garlic cloves
- 3 cup broth or water

Method:

1. Preheat the oven to 425 degrees F.
2. In a mixing dish, combine all of the ingredients for the meatballs.
3. Preheat the oven to 350 degrees Fahrenheit and bake for 15-20 minutes.
4. While the meatballs bake, chop the vegetables and prepare your favourite whole grain.
5. Once the grains and meatballs are done, assemble the plates.

Mediterranean Wild Rice Bowls

❖ **1 hour of cooking time**
❖ **Size of each serving: 4**

Ingredients: Cauliflower Roasted

- 1 tablespoon cumin
- 1 tablespoon sumac
- 1 little head of cauliflower
- 2 tablespoons avocado oil

Rice

- 3 1/2 cup water
- 1 cup uncooked wild rice

Salad

- 1/2 olives Kalamata
- 2 dates (Medjool)
- 1 cup shredded red cabbage
- Two carrots
- 2 chickpea cans (15.5 oz.)
- Cherry tomatoes, 1/2 oz.
- 1 tablespoon of olive oil
- 4 kale leaves

Dressing

- 1 garlic clove
- 1/2 tsp. sea salt
- 2 tbsp. Dijon mustard
- 1 tsp. dried oregano
- three tbsp lemon juice
- 1 tablespoon vinegar (red wine)
- 1/2 cup extra-virgin olive oil

Method:

1. Preheat the oven to 400 degrees F.
2. Bring the wild rice and water to a boil in a 3-quart pot.
3. Turn down the heat and cover.
4. Bake for 55 minutes, or until the veggies are tender.
5. While the rice is cooking, prepare the cauliflower.
6. In a medium mixing bowl, combine sumac, avocado oil, and cumin.
7. Roast for 25 minutes on the prepared baking sheet.
8. In a jar, briskly shake the dressing ingredients.
9. Massage with olive oil for one minute.
10. Prepare the bowls.

Mediterranean Salad with Spicy Yogurt Dressing

❖ **Time to cook: 30 minutes**
❖ **Size of each serving: 4**

Ingredients:

- 1 radish from a watermelon
- a single radish
- 1/2 cup baby kale 1 heirloom carrot
- 1 cup chickpeas, canned
- 1 pound sweet snap peas
- 1 cup uncooked wild rice

Method:

1.   Prepare wild rice according to package recommendations.
2.   In a medium mixing bowl, combine lemon juice, Greek yoghurt, cayenne pepper, salt, spicy sauce, cumin, garlic, and pepper.
3.   Place half of the wild rice in each bowl, followed by the watermelon, snap peas, carrots, kale, chickpeas, and radish.
4.   Top with Spicy Yogurt Sauce and serve immediately.

Mediterranean Grain Bowls with Chickpeas and Lentils

❖ **Time to cook: 10 minutes**
❖ **4 servings**

Ingredients:

- a handful of olives
- Garnish with feta cheese
- two avocados
- 1 cup fresh parsley
- 2 quarts tomatoes
- two shallots
- 2 cups brown lentils
- 2 quarts chickpeas
- 1 corvette
- 2 c. farro
- Salt
- Extra virgin olive oil

Dressing

- 1 tablespoon za'atar
- 1/2 tsp. sumac
- 2 &1/2 teaspoon mustard
- seasoned with salt & pepper
- a third cup of olive oil
- 1 garlic clove
- 2 1/2 tbsp. lemon juice

Method:

1. Heat the olive oil in a nonstick skillet or pan over medium heat.
2. Add the sliced zucchini and sauté until both sides are done.
3. Add a sprinkle of salt to taste.
4. Half-fill a jar with the dressing ingredients.
5. Tightly close the cover and violently shake it.
6. Divide the lentils, cooked farro, and chickpeas equally among four dinner plates.

Mediterranean Mezze Bowl

❖ **Time to Cook: 50 minutes**
❖ **4 servings**

Ingredients: Tabbouleh with Quinoa

- 1 cucumber cup
- 1 1/2 cup cherry tomatoes
- 1 cup parsley, flat-leaf
- 1 cup mint leaves, fresh
- 1 teaspoon ground black pepper
- 1 cup chopped scallions
- 1/4 cup extra virgin olive oil
- 1/2 tsp kosher salt
- 1/4 cup lemon juice (about)
- 1 quinoa cup

Hummus Made Simple

- 1/4 teaspoon black pepper
- three tbsp olive oil
- 1 garlic clove
- 1/2 tsp salt 1/4 cup water
- 1/2 tsp cumin 1/2 cups tahini
- 3 tablespoons fresh lemon juice
- 1 chickpea can

Cucumbers Pickled

- 1/2 tsp red pepper
- 1 cup cucumber
- 4 tablespoons sugar
- 1 tablespoon soy sauce
- 1/4 cup rice vinegar (about)

Vegetables

- two yellow squashes
- 2 roasted red peppers
- 1 Brussels sprouts bag (1/2 oz.)

Method:

1. Combine all of the ingredients except the olive oil in a food processor.
2. Drizzle in the olive oil while mixing.
3. In a small mixing bowl, combine the olive oil, lemon juice, and salt.
4. In a large mixing bowl, combine the cooked quinoa and the lemon juice dressing.
5. Combine the tomatoes, parsley, scallions, cucumber, and pepper in a mixing bowl.
6. Combine all of the ingredients.
7. Gently toss the cucumber slices in the vinegar mixture until evenly coated.
8. Preheat the oven to 400 degrees F.
9. Preheat the oven to 350°F and bake for 30 minutes, or until the veggies are tender but still somewhat crisp.
10. Roast the peppers for 20 minutes under a preheated broiler.

Rotisserie Chicken in a Mediterranean Rice Bowl

❖ **Time to cook: 2 hours**
❖ **Size of each serving: 4**

Ingredients:

- 1/4 teaspoon salt for the salad
- 1/8 teaspoon ground black pepper
- 1 teaspoon olive oil
- 1 lemon juice
- 1/4 cup olives, kalamata
- 1/4 cup feta crumbles
- 2 tomatoes, plum
- 1 pound English cucumber

Regarding the Rice

- 1 pound brown rice
- 2 c. chicken stock

Regarding the Chicken

- 1/8 teaspoon ground black pepper
- 1/4 cup tzatziki dressing
- 1 teaspoon dried oregano
- 1 teaspoon rosemary 1/4 teaspoon salt
- 1 teaspoon fresh thyme
- 1 teaspoon olive oil
- 4 rotisserie chicken cups
- 1 lemon juice
- 1 garlic clove

Method:

1.   In a medium saucepan over high heat, bring the chicken stock and rice to a boil.
2.   Reduce the heat to medium-low and keep cooking.
3.   In a medium mixing bowl, combine the tomatoes, cucumbers, and olives.
4.   Combine the salt, feta, lemon juice, oil, and pepper in a mixing bowl.
5.   Heat the oil in a medium saucepan over medium heat.
6.   Continue to cook, stirring occasionally, until the garlic is aromatic.
7.   Combine the lime juice, chicken, and spices in a mixing bowl.
8.   Cook for another 5 minutes, or until the chicken is well heated.

Grain Bowls with Salmon from the Mediterranean

❖   **Time to cook: 30 minutes**
❖   **6 servings**

Ingredients:

- 1/4 cup fresh basil leaves
- 1 tsp red pepper flakes
- 1/4 cup sliced red onion
- 1 lemon, zest and juice
- 1 avocado, medium
- 1 pound Kalamata olives

- 1 pound 1/2 cup cherry tomatoes
- Black pepper with coarse salt
- 4 oz feta cheese
- 1 pound cucumber
- 6 salmon fillets
- 1/4 cup extra virgin olive oil
- 1/1/2 cup quinoa

Method:

1.   Prepare the quinoa according to the package directions.
2.   Heat the oven to a low boiling temperature.
3.   Place the fish on a baking sheet and bake for 15 minutes.
4.   Drizzle with olive oil and season with salt and black pepper.
5.   Broil for 5-7 minutes, or until golden brown.
6.   Scoop grain into four different dishes to form the bowls.
7.   Arrange the fish and feta slices on top of the quinoa.
8.   Arrange the remaining ingredients, including the cheese, on top.

Mediterranean Edamame Quinoa Bowl

❖ **Cooking Time: 1/2 minutes**
❖ **1 serving size**

Ingredients: Salad Bowl

- 1/4 cup sliced red onions
- 2 teaspoons pine nuts
- 10 olives, Kalamata
- 1 Persian cucumber, tiny
- 2 c. greens
- a 1/2 cup cherry tomatoes
- 1/2 cup quinoa, cooked
- edamame, 1/2 cup

Vinaigrette de la Mediterranean

- 1 tsp. red paprika
- 1/2 teaspoon dried oregano
- a pinch of sea salt a pinch of black pepper
- 1/2 tbsp. red wine vinegar
- 1 garlic clove
- 1 teaspoon olive oil

Method:

1. Arrange the greens on a large plate.
2. Top the greens with cooked quinoa, cherry tomatoes, cucumbers, red onions, Kalamata olives, edamame, and peanuts.
3. Whisk together all of the vinaigrette ingredients.
4. Drizzle the dressing over the salad bowl equally.

Bowl of Mediterranean Hummus with Chickpeas and Soft-Boiled Egg

❖ **Time to cook: 5 minutes**
1 serving size

Ingredients:

- 1 hard-boiled egg
- 1/4 cup salad tabbouleh
- 1/2 cup aborigine
- a 1/2 cup of chickpeas
- a 1/2 cup hummus

Method

1.   Place the hummus in the bottom of a small bowl.
2.   Arrange the chickpeas, egg, eggplant, and tabbouleh salad on top.

Mediterranean Plant Protein Power Bowl

❖ **Time to Cook: 25 minutes**
❖ **2 servings**

Ingredients:

- 1/2 lemon juice
- 1 teaspoon vinegar (red wine)
- 1/2 avocados
- 2 teaspoons olive oil
- 1/2 sliced cucumber
- 1/4 onion, red
- 1/4 cup olives, kalamata
- 1/4 c. hummus
- 2 c. spinach
- a 1/2 cup cherry tomatoes
- 2 cups veggie broth
- 1 cup uncooked quinoa

Method

1. Combine the quinoa and vegetable broth in a large saucepan over medium heat.
2. Bring to a boil, then reduce to a low temperature.
3. Cook for another 10 to 15 minutes, covered, over low heat.
4. Toss together cherry tomatoes, spinach leaves, cucumber, red onion, olives, hummus, avocado, and quinoa in a large mixing bowl.
5. Drizzle with lemon juice, olive oil, and red wine vinegar.

Copy Cat Cava Mediterranean Grain Bowl

❖ **Time to Cook: 15 minutes**
❖ **1 serving**

Ingredients: extra mint

- Lemon Squeeze
- cabbage (25g)
- Hummus (40g)
- Pickled red onion (25g)
- 1/4g feta cheese
- Greek Salsa 100g
- 30-gramme tzatziki
- Arugula (75g)
- Grilled Greek chicken 100g
- a 1/2 cup brown rice

Method

1. Combine brown rice and arugula in a large mixing bowl.
2. Top with hummus, grilled Greek chicken, pickled onion, Greek Salsa, tzatziki, and cabbage.
3. Optional extra mint, feta, and lemon zest.

Mediterranean Salad Dressed in Lemon

❖ **Time to cook: 15 minutes**
❖ **8 servings**

Ingredients:

- 31/2 cup water
- 2 cups of kale
- 2 cups cooked quinoa

Tahini Dressing

- 2 teaspoons water
- Season with salt to taste
- three tbsp lemon juice
- 2 tablespoons olive oil
- 2 tbsp tahini

Protein

- 2 tbsp. Kosher salt
- 1 teaspoon ground black pepper
- 1 teaspoon olive oil

Mediterranean Seasoning Blend

- 1 tbsp cumin 1 tbsp kosher salt
- 3 tbsp dried oregano
- 1 tsp ground red pepper
- Sesame seeds, 3 tbsp.

Fixings

- 1 jar of canned peppers
- a single avocado
- 2 crock-pot cherry tomatoes
- 1 artichoke heart can
- 2 cucumbers, tiny

Method:

1.	Cook the quinoa according to package directions.
2.	Preheat the oven to 400 degrees F.
3.	Line a baking sheet with parchment paper and place the fish on it.
4.	Season both sides of the halibut with salt and pepper, then with the Mediterranean spice blend.
5.	Drizzle the olive oil over the fish.
6.	Bake the salmon for 10 minutes at 350°F.
7.	In a mixing dish, combine all of the dressing ingredients.

Pita Bowls with Mediterranean Chicken and Rice

- ❖	**Time to cook: 20 minutes**
- ❖	**4 servings**

Ingredients:

- 1 chicken cup Lemon wedges
- 1/2 cup onions
- 2 tsp. za'atar 2 tsp. garlic
- 1 teaspoon olive oil
- 1 teaspoon lemon juice
- 1 teaspoon water
- 4 rounds of pita bread
- 2 teaspoons tahini paste
- Nonstick cooking spray

Method:

1. Cook the rice according to the package directions.
2. Preheat the oven to 425 degrees F.
3. Press pitas into oven-safe bowls or cups to form a bowl.
4. Place on a baking sheet and bake for 20 minutes.
5. In a small bowl, combine the lemon juice, water, tahini, and garlic.
6. Continue to stir until the mixture is entirely smooth.
7. Heat the oil in a medium skillet over medium heat.
8. Sauté the remaining garlic and onions for 1 minute.
9. In a mixing dish, combine the chicken, za'atar, and rice.
10. Continue to sauté for another 2 minutes.
11. Half-fill pita plates with rice mixture and tahini sauce.

Panera Mediterranean Warm Grain Bowl Copycat

❖ **Cooking Time: 35 minutes**
❖ **Size of serving: 2**

Ingredients:

- 1/4 cup tahini dressing 1/2 lemon
- 1/3 cup feta cheese
- 1/2 cup plain Greek yoghurt
- 1/2 cucumbers
- a 1/2 cup hummus
- 10 little grape tomatoes
- 3/4cupsp Kalamata olives
- 2 cups brown rice, cooked
- 2 c. arugula
- 2 quarts marinade
- 2 breasts of chicken

Method

1. Marinate the chicken breasts in the Mojo Criollo Marinade overnight.
2. Preheat the oven to 350 degrees Fahrenheit and bake for 20 minutes.
3. Cook the rice/quinoa according to the package directions.
4. Arrange greens along the edge of two big serving plates.
5. Get the veggies ready.
6. Arrange cooked quinoa in two dishes on top of the greens.

7.   Combine the quinoa/greens with cucumber, tomatoes, and olives.

8.   Arrange the chicken pieces over the quinoa.

Quinoa Bowls with Maple Tahini Dressing from the Mediterranean

- ❖   **Time to cook: 25 minutes**
- ❖   **4 servings**

Ingredients:

- 1 tiny red onion for the Quinoa Bowl
- 1/4 cup fresh parsley
- 1 pound English cucumber
- 1-quart cherry tomatoes
- 1 tin black olives
- 1 pound feta cheese
- 2 cups fresh baby spinach
- 1 artichoke heart can
- 2 cups chicken broth
- 1 cup cooked quinoa

Tahini with maple syrup dressing

- 4 tbsp heated water
- Season with salt and pepper to taste.
- 2 tablespoons maple syrup
- 1/2 teaspoon dried oregano
- 1 teaspoon olive oil
- 1 tablespoon vinegar (red wine)
- 1 lemon juice
- 1/4 tbsp tahini

Method:

1.	Cook the quinoa according to package directions.
2.	To make the dressing, combine the lemon juice, extra virgin olive oil, tahini, maple syrup, red wine vinegar, and oregano.
3.	Pour in boiling water one spoonful at a time.
4.	Continue whisking until all of the water has been incorporated into the dressing.
5.	Season to taste with salt and pepper

Chapter 4
Recipes for Greek Bowls

Skinny Greek Chicken Bowls

❖ **Time to cook: 45 minutes**
❖ **Size of each serving: 4**

Ingredients: Chicken Ingredients

- Seasoned with salt & pepper
- 2 cups riced cauliflower
- a 1/2 teaspoon basil
- 3/4cupsp yoghurt
- 1teaspoonson dried oregano
- teaspoon fresh thyme
- 2 teaspoons minced garlic
- 1/4 cup lemon juice (about)
- 2-pound chicken tenders

Toppings

- 1/2 cucumbers, English
- Tzatziki Sauce 1/2 cup
- 1 cup sliced tomatoes
- 1/2 cup sliced red onion
- 2 romaine lettuce cups

Method:

1.	In a large mixing basin, combine the diced chicken.
2.	Stir in the Greek yoghurt, garlic, spices, salt, lemon juice, and pepper until the chicken is thoroughly coated.
3.	Grill or bake the chopped chicken until it is lightly browned.
4.	Assemble the bowls: Place cooked rice or quinoa in each of the four dishes.
5.	Cooked diced grilled chicken and other toppings are placed on top.

Greek Goddess Bulgur Bowls

- ❖ **Time to cook: 30 minutes**
- ❖ **2 servings**

Ingredients:

- Pepper
- 2 tsp vegetable oil
- a 1/2 cup hummus
- Salt
- 4 oz. grape tomatoes
- 1 cup Greek vinaigrette
- 1 pound red onion
- 1/2 cup buckwheat bulgur
- 1/4 oz. dill
- 1/2 c. feta cheese
- 1 tbsp harissa powder
- 1 pound Persian cucumber
- Chickpeas (1/3.4 oz.)

Method:

1. Toss chopped onion and chickpeas with a generous drizzle of oil, harissa powder, and salt on a baking sheet.
2. Roast on the top rack until the onion is caramelised and the chickpeas are lightly browned.
3. Meanwhile, in a small saucepan, combine the harissa powder, bulgur, water, and salt.
4. Heat to a boil, then reduce to low heat and cover.
5. In a medium mixing bowl, combine half of the chopped dill, tomatoes, cucumber, and half of the Greek vinaigrette.

6.	Distribute the bulgur among the serving dishes.
7.	Arrange the roasted onion and chickpeas on top, followed by the cucumber feta salad.

Greek Chicken and Potato Bowl

❖	**Cooking Time: 6 hours 65 minutes for 4.3**
❖	**4 servings**

Ingredients:

- 1 tsp kosher salt
- 1 tbsp olive oil
- 1/4 cup extra virgin olive oil
- 2 potatoes, russet
- 4 garlic cloves
- 1 lemon, big
- 1/4 tsp red pepper flakes
- 1 tsp cayenne pepper
- 1 teaspoon fresh thyme
- 2 tsp dried oregano
- 2 tsp ground black pepper
- 1 teaspoon thyme
- 2 tbsp. kosher salt
- 2 lbs chicken thighs
- To make the Salad
- 1 pound feta cheese
- 4 cups mixed salad greens
- 2 crock-pot cherry tomatoes
- 1/2 cup sliced red onion
- 2 cups cucumber (English)

To make the dressing

- 2 teaspoons fresh parsley
- 2 tbsp dried oregano
- 1 lemon, big
- Black pepper with salt
- 1 / 3 cup olive oil
- 1/4 cup vinegar (red wine)

Method

1. In a large mixing bowl, combine the oregano, chicken thighs, rosemary, sea salt, pepper, thyme, cayenne, garlic, lemon juice, red pepper flakes, and olive oil.
2. Heat the oven to 475 degrees Fahrenheit.
3. Arrange the chicken thighs on a baking sheet.
4. Roast in the centre of a preheated oven until the meat is cooked through.
5. While the meat and potatoes are cooking, mix the dressing ingredients: salt, olive oil, lemon juice, red wine vinegar, and pepper.
6. Using a spatula, remove the potatoes once they have cooled for a few minutes.

Lunch Bowls with Greek Chicken Salad

❖ **Time to cook: 15 minutes**
❖ **5 servings**

Ingredients: For the Bowls

- 1 medium cucumber
- 1 cup sliced cherry tomatoes
- 1/2 cup feta cheese
- kalamata olives (23 cups)
- 1 hummus cup
- 1 tbsp. tzatziki
- 4 c. chicken
- 6 cups fresh baby spinach

To make the Greek Dressing

- 1 tsp fine sea salt
- 1/4 tsp black pepper
- 1/1/2 teaspoon oregano
- 1 tsp. garlic powder
- 1/2 cup extra-virgin olive oil
- 1 1/2 tsp basil 2 tbsp red wine vinegar
- three tbsp lemon juice

Method:

1.   To make the dressing, put all of the ingredients in a mason jar.
2.   Fill five lunch containers halfway with mixed greens, then divide the tzatziki, hummus, feta, chicken, cucumber, olives, and tomatoes evenly.
3.   Store in the refrigerator for up to five days before serving.

Instant Pot Greek Chicken Rice Bowl

❖   **Time to Cook:**
❖   **4 Servings**

Ingredients: For the Chicken Bowl

- 1 cup cooked chicken breast
- 1 teaspoon ground pepper, lemon
- 1/4 tsp of salt
- 1/8 teaspoon ground black pepper
- 1 teaspoon dried oregano
- 1 garlic clove
- 1 cup chicken stock
- 1/2 cup uncooked white rice
- 1 tablespoon melted butter
- Lemon juice with zest
- 1 teaspoon olive oil

To make the Tzatziki Sauce

- a quarter teaspoon garlic
- 1 tablespoon of olive oil

- 1/16 teaspoon ground black pepper
- 1 teaspoon lemon juice 1/4 teaspoons dill
- 3 tbsp cucumber, 1/8 teaspoon salt
- 4 1/2 tbsp yoghurt

For the icing

- 2 tbsp. red onion 2 tbsp. cucumber
- 2 tbsp. roasted red bell pepper
- 2 tbsp of feta cheese
- 2 tbsp Kalamata olives
- 2 tablespoons tomato sauce

1. **Method**:

1. In a bowl dish or jar, combine all sauce ingredients and refrigerate until ready to use.

2. To make the Chicken Bowl, combine the lemon juice, butter, oil, zest, broth, salt, oregano, rice, garlic, and black pepper.

3. In a small dish, toss the chicken with the lemon pepper, then spread it evenly over the rice.

4. Divide the chicken and rice evenly in a serving dish, then top with the bell pepper, onion, feta, cucumber, tomatoes, and olives.

5. Serve immediately with tzatziki sauce.

Greek Chickpea Salad with Marinated Chickpeas

- ❖ **Time to cook: 25 minutes**
- ❖ **2 servings**

Ingredients: Chickpeas Marinated

- 1/4 tsp of salt
- a pinch of ground black pepper
- 1/2 cup roasted red peppers
- 1 teaspoon dried oregano
- 1/2 lemons, tiny
- 3 garlic cloves
- 1/4 cup extra virgin olive oil
- 1/4 tsp fresh parsley 1/4 tbsp red wine vinegar
- 1 15-ounce can chickpeas

Toppings for the Bowl

- Lemon juice
- White Rice
- Tzatziki sauce prepared from scratch
- Pita chips with garlic and herbs
- 1/2 c. feta cheese
- 1 cup sliced cherry tomatoes
- 1/2 cucumbers, English

Method:

1. Half-fill a bowl with chickpeas.
2. Squeeze the lemon over the parsley, garlic, and roasted red peppers.
3. In a mixing bowl, combine the olive oil, red wine vinegar, and spices.
4. Season to taste, adding salt as necessary.
5. When everything is ready, assemble the bowl!

The Greek Lentil Power Bowl

❖ **Time to cook: 40 minutes**
❖ **Size of serving: 3**

Ingredients:

- 1/4 cup feta cheese
- Season with salt and pepper to taste.
- 1/4 cup sliced red onion
- a 1/2 cup of chickpeas
- a 1/2 cup cucumber
- a 1/2 cup cherry tomatoes
- 1 teaspoon lemon juice
- 1 tablespoon honey
- 1 cup cooked brown lentils
- 1/4 cup yoghurt (Greek)
- 1 teaspoon dill
- 2 cups of water

Method:

1. Bring the water, lentils, and salt to a boil in a saucepan.
2. After the water has reached a boil, cover and reduce the heat to low.
3. Cook for 35 minutes, or until the water is completely absorbed.
4. While the lentils are cooking, combine the dill, lemon juice, Greek yoghurt, and honey in a separate dish.
5. After stirring with a spoon, set away.
6. Serve with a side of Greek yoghurt dressing.

Greek Salmon Bowl

- ❖ **Time to cook: 42 minutes**
- ❖ **Size of each serving: 4**

Ingredients:
Bowl

- 1/2 c. feta cheese
- a single avocado
- 1 garbanzo bean can
- 1 kalamata olive (1/3 cups)
- 1 cup sliced tomatoes
- 1/2 cup sliced red onion
- 4 cups romaine lettuce
- 1 cup cucumber (English)
- 1 pound cooked quinoa
- 4 fillets of salmon

Marinade

- 1/2 tsp sea salt 1/4 tsp black pepper
- 2 garlic cloves
- 1 tablespoon honey
- 2 tbsp oregano (leaves)
- 1 tablespoon dill, fresh
- 1 tangerine
- 1/2 cup extra-virgin olive oil

Tzatziki

- 1/4 teaspoon sea salt
- 1/4 teaspoons black pepper
- 1 tbsp fresh dill 2 garlic cloves
- 1/2 teaspoon lemon juice
- 1 teaspoon olive oil
- 1/2 cup plain Greek yoghurt
- 1/2 cup cucumber (English)

Method:

1.   Preheat the oven to 450 degrees F.
2.   In a mixing dish, combine the marinade ingredients.
3.   Place the fish in a shallow dish.
4.   Pour half of the marinade over the salmon and set aside for fifteen minutes to marinate.
5.   Bake in a preheated oven for 9-1/2 minutes.
6.   In a mixing bowl, combine the cherry tomatoes, red onion, cucumber slices, and garbanzo beans.
7.   Stir in the remaining marinade.
8.   Combine all of the Tzatziki sauce ingredients in a mixing dish and gently swirl to combine.
9.   Create a group of four or five bowls.

Chapter 5
Recipes for Lebanese Bowls

Tahini Drizzled Lebanese Buddha Bowl

❖　　　**Time to cook: 30 minutes**
❖　　　**Size of each serving: 4**

Ingredients: **Regarding the Beetroot Couscous**

- 2 tbsp. fresh lemon juice
- To taste, black pepper
- 2 cooked beets, tiny
- 1 teaspoon powdered bouillon
- 240ml of water
- Couscous (100g)

Regarding the Falafel

- Pinch of black pepper
- toasted sesame seeds
- 1 teaspoon coriander
- 2 tbsp of aquafaba
- four tbsp breadcrumbs

- 1 tsp parsley
- 1 teaspoon cumin
- 1 teaspoon tahini
- 400g canned chickpeas
- 1 medium onion
- 2 garlic cloves

To make the Tahini Dressing

- A small amount of water
- Pinch of black pepper
- 1 garlic clove
- 1 tangerine
- 4 teaspoons tahini

Method:

1. Combine the big grains, beetroot, water, and bouillon in a saucepan and slowly boil for the couscous.
2. Cook for a further 8 minutes.
3. After seasoning with lemon and black pepper, set aside to chill.
4. Preheat the oven to 180° Celsius.
5. In a food processor, combine all of the falafel ingredients except the sesame seeds.
6. Form golf ball-sized amounts of the falafel paste into balls or patties using wet hands.
7. Preheat the oven to 350°F and bake for 30 minutes.
8. Arrange a few falafel pieces on top of some of the couscous.

Bowls of Lebanese Falafel

❖   **Time to cook: 24 minutes**
❖   **Size of each serving: 4**

Ingredients: Dressing with a zesty tahini

- The pita bread
- 1/4 cup feta cheese
- 1/4 cup onion
- 1/4 cup harissa 1/2 cup tzatziki
- 2 cups salad (Israeli)
- a 1/2 cup hummus
- 1 purple cabbage cup
- 1 falafel batch
- 2 quarts brown rice
- 4 cups fresh baby spinach

Method:

1.   Make ahead of time all of the falafel, Israeli salad, hummus, tzatziki, and tahini dressing.
2.   Divide the white rice, baby spinach, and purple cabbage into three separate bowls.
3.   To each bowl, combine 3-4 cooked harissa, falafel patties, tzatziki, feta, Israeli salad, hummus, and pickled onions.

Lebanese Vegetarian Bowl

❖ **Cooking Time: 30 minutes**
❖ **4 Servings**

Ingredients: Tahini Rice Salad

- 1 onion (spring)
- Pomegranate seeds (40g)
- 1 tbsp. tamari
- 2 tbsp natural yoghurt
- 2 tbsp. tahini
- 100 grammes brown rice

Chickpeas with Spices

- four radishes
- 2 slices of lemon
- Hummus with 2 red peppers
- a single avocado
- 2 bunches salad leaves
- 10 medium green olives
- 1 tablespoon cumin
- 1 tablespoon paprika
- 0.5 teaspoon turmeric, pinch salt
- 1 teaspoon olive oil
- 1 tin chickpeas (400g)

Method:

1.   Prepare the brown rice according to package instructions.

2.	Stir in the pomegranate seeds and spring onion, then set aside.

3.	To make the spiced chickpeas, drain the canned chickpeas and put them in a medium saucepan with paprika, salt, cumin, olive oil, and turmeric.

1.	Cook for 5 minutes on medium-high heat!

4.	At this step, construct the two Buddha bowls.

Lebanese Bean Salad Bowl

❖	**Cooking Time: 23 minutes**
❖	**4 servings**

Ingredients: Salad Bowls with Lebanese Beans

- 1 can of bean salad
- 1/2 cup ready-made hummus
- 1/8 teaspoon each of salt and pepper
- 1/4 cup parsley, fresh
- 1 couscous cup
- 1/4 cup shallots 1 cup vegetable broth
- 1 teaspoon olive oil

Lemon and parsley dressing

- 1/2 tsp Dijon mustard
- 1/4 cup extra virgin olive oil
- 1/2 teaspoon of salt
- 1/4 teaspoon black pepper
- 1 lemon, big
- 1 garlic clove, tiny
- 1/2 cup fresh parsley

Method

1. Heat the oil in a small saucepan over medium-high heat.
2. Cook for another 2-3 minutes after adding the shallots.
3. Cook for 1 minute more, or until the couscous is lightly browned.
4. Bring the stock and salt to a boil, then turn off the heat.
5. Whisk together the lemon juice/zest, pepper, parsley, salt, garlic, and mustard in a small bowl until the mustard is mixed.
6. If desired, season with salt and pepper to taste.
7. Toss the couscous with the dressing.
8. Make the bowls.

Bowls of Lebanese Cauliflower

- ❖ **1 hour of cooking time**
- ❖ **4 servings**

Ingredients: For the Baba Ganoush

- 1 teaspoon cumin powder
- Juice 1 tangerine
- 1/2 teaspoon tahini
- 1/2 teaspoon chilli powder
- 1/2 tbsp. olive oil
- 2 cloves garlic
- 2 aubergines, big

Cauliflower as a side dish

- 1/2 oz olive oil
- Juice 1/2 lemon
- 1/2 tbsp. shawarma spice blend
- Cauliflower florets (600g)

To make the Tabbouleh

- 2 green onions
- Pomegranate seeds (50g)
- 3 ripe tomatoes
- 1 cup cucumber
- a large bunch of parsley
- a little handful of mint
- three tbsp olive oil
- Juice 1/2 lemons
- 400g canned chickpeas
- 100g wheat bulgur

Method:

1. Preheat the oven to 200° Celsius.

2.	In a large roasting pan, combine the spice blend, cauliflower, and seasonings.

3.	Drizzle with olive oil and roast for 30 minutes, or until the veggies are just tender.

4.	Keep the lemon juice that has been squeezed over it aside.

5.	Prepare the baba ganoush in the meantime.

6.	Season to taste with salt and pepper, then set aside.

7.	In a medium saucepan, bring the bulgur wheat and water to a boil.

8.	Cover and simmer for 8-10 minutes.

9.	Combine the remaining tabbouleh ingredients, as well as a liberal quantity of spice, in a mixing bowl.

Lebanese Ground Beef Bowl

- ❖	**Cooking Time: 20 minutes**
- ❖	**6 servings**

Ingredients:

- 1/2 tsp. mint leaves 1/4 tsp. ginger
- 1 teaspoon ground allspice
- 1/2 tsp cayenne pepper
- 2 tablespoons cumin
- 1/1/2 teaspoon cinnamon
- 1/4 cups of water
- 2 tbsp coriander (cilantro)
- 1 tsp Kosher salt
- 1/2 tsp black pepper
- 1 medium yellow onion
- 4 garlic cloves
- 2 lbs. beef

Method

1.   In a large skillet over medium-high heat, combine the onion, ground beef, salt, and pepper.
2.   Brown the meat in batches, breaking it up as you go.
3.   In a small cup, combine the water, cayenne pepper, cumin, mint leaves, cinnamon, coriander, allspice, and ginger.
4.   Trim away any excess fat before adding the seasonings.
5.   Cook, stirring regularly until the water has evaporated.

Tahini Yogurt Tahini

❖   **Time to cook: 8 hours 40 minutes**
❖   **Servings per recipe: 6**

Ingredients: Yoghurt Tahini Sauce

- Season with salt and pepper to taste.
- 1/2 cups of water
- 1 clove garlic
- 1/2 lemon
- 1/2 cup yoghurt
- 1/2 tbsp tahini paste

Falafel

- 1/2 tsp baking powder
- Grapeseed oil (vegetable)
- three tbsp flour
- 1 tsp. baking soda
- 1/2 tsp cayenne pepper
- 2 tablespoons cumin
- 2 tbsp. kosher salt
- 1 tablespoon fresh coriander
- 1 bundle fresh parsley
- 1 bunch coriander
- 1 onion, yellow
- 4 cloves garlic
- 2 quarts chickpeas

Homemade Hummus in a Falafel Bowl

- Extra virgin olive oil
- Oregano, dried
- Zaatar
- Feta cubes
- Greens for salad Arugula

Israeli Salad with Chops

- 1 to 2 tbsp lemon juice
- Extra virgin olive oil
- 1 tablespoon dried mint
- 1/2 tsp Kosher salt
- TWO TOMATOES
- Persian cucumbers, 2

Method

1.   Soak the dried chickpeas in a large basin of water.

2.   Drain chickpeas and pulse in a food processor until finely smashed, then transfer to a large mixing bowl and set aside.

3.   In the same food processor, pulse the onion, herbs, garlic, and spices until finely ground, then add the herb mixture to the crushed chickpeas.

4.   In a mixing basin, combine the baking soda, flour, and baking powder.

5.   In the meantime, heat the vegetable oil in a large pan.

6.   Fry 4-6 falafel till golden brown on both sides, approximately 3-5 minutes on each side.

7.   In a small food processor, add all of the tahini yoghurt sauce ingredients and pulse until smooth.

Bowl of Braised Lebanese Lentil Freekeh

- ❖ **Time to cook: 35 minutes**
- ❖ **Servings per container: 10**

Ingredients:

- 1 teaspoon black pepper
- 1/4 cup lemon juice 20 oz. black forest ham
- 2 tsp cayenne pepper
- 4 c. kale
- three tbsp canola oil
- a third cup of pine nuts
- 1 cup roasted red bell peppers
- a 1/2 cup currants
- 2 quarts beef broth
- 2 cups quinoa
- 1/4 teaspoon cinnamon
- 1/2 cup lentils

Method

1. In a slow cooker, combine cinnamon, lentils, currants, freekeh, and stock.
2. Cook on high for 35 minutes.
3. In a mixing bowl, combine pine nuts, oil, kale, lemon juice, cayenne pepper, red pepper, and pepper.
4. Gently soften and wilt the greens.
5. Arrange each portion on a plate and top with sliced ham.

Chapter 6
Recipes for Vegetarian Bowls

Ratatouille Buckwheat with Burrata Bowl

- ❖ **1 hour of cooking time**
- ❖ **6 servings**

Ingredients: Ratatouille in French

- 4 sprigs thyme
- Black pepper with salt
- 5 medium-sized tomatoes
- 1 teaspoon tomato paste
- 1 onion, yellow
- 5 cloves garlic
- 3 bell peppers 2 zucchinis
- Olive oil (extra virgin)
- 1 medium eggplant

Additional Ingredients

- a dash of salt
- 2 burrata balls, fresh
- 3 1/2 cups water
- 2 buckwheat cups

Method:

1. Heat about three tablespoons of olive oil in a large nonstick pan over medium heat.
2. Cook the zucchini, eggplants, and bell peppers separately until soft and beginning to brown.
3. Add another tablespoon of oil, then the onion and tomato paste.
4. Cook for roughly 5 minutes on medium heat.
5. After adding the cooked zucchini, eggplant, and bell peppers to the pan, simmer for 10 to 15 minutes.
6. Bring 3 cups of water to a boil in a kettle or saucepan with a pinch of salt.
7. 2 cups buckwheat, mixed in and returned to a boil
8. Divide the buckwheat among the serving dishes, then top with the ratatouille.

Abundance Bowl Spring

❖ **Cooking Time for the Bowl: 40 minutes**
❖ **4 servings**

Ingredients: Dressing in Meyer Lemon and Shallots

- 1 tablespoon Dijon mustard
- four tbsp olive oil
- 1 1/2 cup Meyer lemon juice
- 1/2 teaspoon of salt
- 1 lemon, Meyer
- 1 scallion
- 1 tiny beet

For the bowl

- 1 heaping tablespoon hemp seeds
- 1 avocado, ripe
- a cup of pea shoots
- 1 bay leaf, tiny
- 4 oz. goat cheese
- 1 pound lentils
- 1 garlic clove
- 1/2 teaspoon of salt
- 1 quinoa cup

Method:

1. Combine all of the ingredients in a container.
2. In a small saucepan, mix water, quinoa, and salt over medium-high heat.
3. Bring to a boil, then decrease the heat to low.

4.	Place the lentils in a small saucepan.
5.	Add two inches of water to the container.
6.	Combine the garlic and bay leaf in a separate bowl.
7.	Cook for 20-25 minutes over medium heat.
8.	Using a slotted spoon, remove the bay leaf and garlic cloves, drain, and set aside.
9.	Divide the hot quinoa and lentils into four dishes.

Pistachio Cashew Cheese Ancient Grain Bowls

❖	**Time to cook: 30 minutes**
❖	**Size of serving: 2**

Ingredients: 4 ounces baby arugula

- 1 teaspoon olive oil
- 1 tangerine
- a single apple
- pistachios (about 2 tbsp)
- cashew cheese, 2 oz.
- two tbsp vegan butter
- 2 oz. leeks, sliced
- 1 tbsp mustard and herb combination

Method:

1. Preheat the oven to 425 degrees F.
2. Heat water, barley, and a bit of salt in a medium saucepan over high heat.
3. Bring to a boil, then lower to low heat and cook for 25 minutes.
4. Combine the French mustard & herb mixture, olive oil, chickpeas, and a pinch of salt on a baking sheet. 10 - 15 minutes, or until somewhat caramelised and crispy.
5. Melt butter in a large nonstick pan over low heat.
6. Season with salt and pepper and add the leeks.
7. Chop the pistachios finely and season with salt and pepper.
8. In a medium mixing bowl, combine the lemon juice, apple slices, arugula, olive oil, and salt and pepper to taste.
9. Combine the arugula and apple salad.

Bowl of Lentil Salad with Sweet Peppers and Basil

❖ **Time to cook: 30 minutes**
❖ **4 Servings**

Ingredients:
Salad

- 1 avocado, large
- 1/2 cup basil, fresh
- 1/3 cup sweet
- 1 sour bell pepper
- 4 cups lentils, green

Dressing

- 1 tablespoon chilli powder
- 1/2 tsp. sea salt
- 2 teaspoons lemon juice
- 2 teaspoons olive oil

Method:

1.   In a large mixing bowl, add all of the salad components and gently toss to incorporate.
2.   In a small mixing bowl, whisk together all of the dressing ingredients.
3.   Toss the salad with the dressing and toss lightly to incorporate.
4.   Fill bowls with the mixture and serve at room temperature, or cover and chill for two or more hours to serve cold.

Farro Bowl with Kale & Figs

❖   **Time to cook: 20 minutes**
❖   **2 servings**

Ingredients:

- 2 tablespoons walnuts
- 2 ounces goat cheese
- 2 large handfuls of kale
- 4 figs
- 1 ½ cups cooked farro

Balsamic Maple Mustard Dressing

- ½ teaspoon kosher salt
- 1/4 teaspoon black pepper
- 2 teaspoons maple syrup
- 1 teaspoon mustard
- 2 tablespoons balsamic
- 2 teaspoons olive oil

Method:

1.   In a small mixing bowl, combine the dressing ingredients.
2.   Divide farro between two bowls.
3.   Massage kale in a mixing bowl with a sprinkle of salt and a drizzle of olive oil until it is covered and malleable.
4.   Divide the kale amongst the dishes.
5.   Add the figs and goat cheese over the top.

Instant Pot Burrito Bowls with Black Beans and Brown Rice

❖ **Cooking Time: 1 hour 10 minutes**
❖ **Size of each serving: 4**

Ingredients: Corn Salsa

- 2 tablespoons cilantro
- ½ jalapeno juice of 1 lime
- 2 tablespoons red onion
- 2 ears corn

Brown Rice

- Juice of ½ lime
- 1/8 cup cilantro
- 1/2 tsp. sea salt
- 1 bay leaf
- 1 cup water
- 1 cup brown rice

Beans, black

- 1/4 teaspoon sea salt 1 lime juice
- 1 tbsp dried oregano
- 1 teaspoon cumin
- 4 c. water
- ONE BAY LEAF
- 3 garlic cloves
- 2 cups dried black beans
- 1 onion, yellow
- 1 tablespoon of olive oil

Other Add-Ons

- 1 guacamole cup
- 1-quart salsa
- 1 Romaine lettuce heart

Method

1.   Heat the oil, if used, in an Instant Pot on sauté mode.
2.   Cook the onion until it is tender.
3.   In a large mixing bowl, combine the bay leaf, oregano, water, cumin, beans, and salt.
4.   In a mixing dish, combine the salt, water, rice, and bay leaf.
5.   Place the rice dish on a trivet on top of the beans.
6.   The rice will steam as the beans cook.
7.   Squeeze lime juice on top of the rice and beans.
8.   Season to taste with salt and pepper.

Acai Bowls

❖   **Time to cook: 5 minutes**
❖   **2 servings**

Ingredients:

- 1/4 cup bananas
- 2 mint sprigs
- 1/4 cups of granola
- 1/4 cup berries, fresh
- 1 frozen fruit cup
- 1 ripe banana
- 7 fluid ounces Acai frozen

Method:

1.   Break up the frozen acai into large pieces while it is still in the packaging.
2.   Place the frozen fruit, frozen acai pieces, and frozen banana in a food processor.
3.   Alternatively, combine the ingredients with a little juice in a blender.
4.   Top the mixed mixture in a dish or bowl with granola and fresh fruit.

Pitaya Bowl

❖ **Cooking Time: 7 minutes**
❖ **1 serving**

Ingredients:

- Kiwi chunks
- Shreds of coconut
- Berries
- Sliced bananas
- Hemp seedlings
- Granola
- a third cup of coconut water
- Chia seeds
- 1 frozen pack Pitaya

Method:

1.   Using your hands, break up the frozen pitaya into pieces.
2.   Stir in any remaining frozen fruit and a little quantity of liquid.
3.   Blend until everything is well combined.
4.   Half-fill a bowl with the frozen mixture and top with your favourite toppings.

Taco Bowls with Quinoa

- ❖ **Time to cook: 20 minutes**
- ❖ **Size of each serving: 4**

Ingredients: Taco Bowls with Quinoa

- Tortilla Chips
- Tortillas
- Store-Bought Guacamole in a Hurry Salsa
- 3 tomatoes, Roma
- 1 coriander
- 1 tin pinto beans
- 1 head of romaine lettuce
- 1 tin black beans
- 2 cups quinoa, cooked
- 1 lime for

Easy guacamole

- garlic salt
- 1 lime juice
- 2 ripe avocados, big

Method

1.   Heat the olive oil in a large pan over medium heat.
2.   Cook until the beans are cooked through.
3.   Taco seasoning can be applied to taste.
4.   Arrange quinoa, tomatoes, lettuce, cilantro, seasoned beans, salsa, cheese, guacamole, and chips or tortillas on the table.
5.   Mash the avocados with lime juice in a small bowl.
6.   Season with garlic salt to taste.

Chili-Orange Veggie Bowl

- ❖   **1 hour to cook**
- ❖   **2 servings**

Ingredients:

- EVOO (extra-virgin olive oil)
- seasoned with salt & pepper
- a little handful of sprouts
- Sesame seeds are sprinkled on top.
- 1/4 cup pomegranate seeds a couple of tofu slabs
- 1 broccoli bunch
- 2 carrots, tiny
- 1 pound sweet potato
- a couple of scallions
- a 1/2 cup rice

Vinaigrette de Chili-Orange

- 1 tsp chilli powder
- 1 teaspoon vinegar (rice)
- 1 tablespoon soy sauce
- 1 tbsp sesame oil
- two tbsp orange juice

Method:

1. Prepare the rice according to the instructions on the rice cooker.
2. Make use of a shallow skillet.
3. Place the sweet potatoes and broccoli in separate steamer trays.
4. Sprinkle with scallions and season with salt and pepper to taste.
5. Next, prepare the dressing and set it aside.
6. Toss carrot ribbons with a dash of rice vinegar and a sprinkle of salt.
7. Allow marinating in the fridge until ready to use.
8. Heat the oil in a pan, then add the tofu and fry on each side.

Roasted Veggie Winter Bliss Bowl

- ❖ **Cooking Time: 30 minutes**
- ❖ **2 servings**

Ingredients:

- Extra virgin olive oil
- 1/4 red onion, seasoned with salt and black pepper
- a little handful of mushrooms
- 1 cup roasted butternut squash
- Green beans, a handful
- 1/2 oz. yellow bell pepper
- 10 little cherry tomatoes
- 1 pound Brussels sprouts
- 2 slender beets
- 1 cup lentils de France
- 2 cups quinoa (red)

Tahini Dressing

- 1/2 lemon juice
- 1/4 cup tahini

Method:

1.	Preheat the oven to 375 degrees F.
2.	Toss the vegetables in a big amount of olive oil and season with salt and pepper.
3.	Arrange on a baking sheet in a single layer and roast for 20 minutes.
4.	Thin the tahini and lemon with enough water to get a dripping consistency.
5.	Divide the hot quinoa and lentils into two bowls.

6. Arrange the roasted vegetables on top.

Vegetarian Chili Bowl

- ❖ **Time to Cook: 30 minutes**
- ❖ **Size of each serving: 4**

Ingredients: To make the pickled onions

- a generous teaspoon of kosher salt
- a little teaspoon of sugar
- 1 onion, red
- a single lime

To make the Chili

- salt kosher
- cilantro, fresh
- 2 cans of black beans
- 1 can (15 oz.) tomatoes
- 1 tablespoon chilli powder
- 1 teaspoon dried oregano
- 1 medium onion
- 3 cloves garlic
- Extra virgin olive oil

Method:

1.   Combine the lime juice, onion, salt, and sugar in a mixing bowl.
2.   Heat the oil in a large skillet over medium-high heat. Fill the container halfway with oil.
3.   When the pan is hot, add the onion and simmer for about five minutes, or until softened.
4.   Cook for another 1 to 2 minutes, or until the chilli powder, garlic, and oregano are fragrant.
5.   Add the beans and tomatoes, along with a few generous pinches of salt, and simmer until the tomatoes have broken down.
6.   Season with more chilli powder, salt, and oregano to taste.

Lentil Bowls with Fried Eggs and Greens

❖ **Time to cook: 40 minutes**
❖ **4 servings**

Ingredients:

- 2 tablespoons olive oil
- four huge eggs
- 1/2 ripe green olives
- a single avocado
- 4 cups fresh baby spinach
- 1 cup red bell peppers
- 1/4 teaspoon black pepper
- 8 c. kale
- 1 teaspoon lemon juice
- 1/2 teaspoon of salt
- 1/4 cup yoghurt (Greek)
- 1 tsp lemon juice
- 2 1/2 cup water
- 2 garlic cloves
- ONE BAY LEAF
- 1/2 c. green lentils

Method

1.   Bring water to a boil in a medium saucepan over high heat.
2.   Combine the smashed garlic, lentils, and bay leaf in a mixing bowl.
3.   Cover and simmer for 25 to 30 minutes, or until the lentils are tender.

4.   In a large mixing bowl, combine the pepper, yoghurt, salt, lemon juice, lemon zest, and minced garlic.
5.   Toss in the spinach and greens to coat.
6.   Divide the kale mixture among four dinner plates and top with roasted red peppers.
7.   Heat the oil in a large nonstick skillet over medium-high heat.
8.   Crack the eggs one at a time into the pan.
9.   Garnish each dish with an egg.

Italian Vegetable Rice Bowl

- ❖ **Cooking Time: 25 minutes**
- ❖ **1 serving size**

Ingredients:

- Extra virgin olive oil
- 2 tbsp white wine vinegar
- seasoned with salt & pepper
- Parsley
- 1 cup parmesan cheese
- 1 1/2 oz. parmesan
- 8 tiny artichokes
- 2 teaspoons lemon juice
- 1 tablespoon melted butter
- 6 cups vegetable broth
- 1 scallion
- 1 garlic clove
- 1 2/3 cup risotto

Method:

1.   Heat the olive oil in a skillet and sauté the shallots and rice until translucent.
2.   Gently fold in the garlic and stock.
3.   Meanwhile, cut the artichokes.
4.   Cook for 7 minutes in a large pot of boiling water.
5.   Just before serving, stir in the parmesan cheese and season with salt and pepper to taste.
6.   Heat the oil in a deep fryer and gently cook the artichokes.
7.   Reduce the heat and season to taste with salt and pepper.

Grilled Veggie Bowl

❖   **Time to Cook: 35 minutes**
❖   **Size of each serving: 4**

Ingredients: Dressing in lemon

- 1 teaspoon dried oregano
- Black pepper with kosher salt
- 1/2 tsp Dijon mustard
- 2 garlic cloves
- 1/3 cup vinegar (red wine)
- 2 teaspoons lemon juice
- 1/2 cup extra-virgin olive oil

Vegetables Grilled

- Extra virgin olive oil
- Black pepper with salt
- 2 medium green bell peppers
- 8 oz. mushrooms
- 1 red onion 2 medium zucchinis

Bowls

- Black pepper with salt
- Pita bread or pita chips
- 1/2 c. feta cheese
- Dill and basil, fresh
- 1 grape tomato cup
- 1 pound Kalamata olives
- Chickpeas (15 oz.)
- 1 cup cucumber
- 2 cups farro cooked

Method:

1. Preheat the grill to high.
2. After sprinkling the vegetables with olive oil, season them with salt and pepper.
3. Preheat the grill.
4. To create the dressing, whisk together the red wine vinegar, olive oil, salt, Dijon mustard, oregano, lemon juice, garlic, and black pepper.
5. Before assembling the bowls, coarsely chop the grilled vegetables.
6. Divide the farro into four dishes and top each with the steaming vegetables.

Veggie Nourish Bowl

❖ **Preparation Time: 1 hour**
❖ **4 servings**

Ingredients:

- 2 cucumbers, tiny
- two avocados
- 1 pound could corn
- 1 pound black beans
- 1 acorn squash and 2 bunches of baby broccoli
- 2 tbsp. sesame oil
- 1 tablespoon miso
- 1 tablespoon cumin
- 1/2 tsp curry powder
- Pinch of black pepper
- 1 cauliflower head
- 1/2 tsp onion powder
- salt kosher
- 1 tablespoon paprika
- 1 tsp. garlic powder
- four potatoes
- 1 teaspoon seasoning with Italian herbs
- three tbsp olive oil

Method

1. Preheat the oven to 400 degrees Fahrenheit.
2. Toss the potatoes with the seasonings.
3. Season the cauliflower with spices.
4. Add to the pan with the potatoes.
5. In a mixing dish, combine sesame oil and miso.

6.   Bake the cauliflower for 30 minutes, or until golden brown.

7.   In the meantime, bring a pot of water to a boil.

8.   Blanch the young broccoli for three minutes.

9.   Heat a dry skillet over medium heat.

10.   Sear the corn kernels for a few minutes.

11.   To serve, divide the ingredients between two plates.

Veggie Burrito Bowl with Brilliant Balance

❖   **Time to cook: 30 minutes**
❖   **Size of each serving: 4**

Ingredients:

- 1 onion (spring)
- a single lime
- 5.5g vegetable stock powder
- cherry tomatoes (1/25g)
- 5 grammes coriander
- 100 grammes brown rice
- 1 cup unsweetened yoghurt
- 1 sachet chipotle paste
- 1 red bell pepper
- 2 tsp. smoked paprika
- 1 sachet tomato paste
- 1 tsp yellow pepper
- 1 tin black beans
- 1 onion, red

Method

1.   Preheat the oven to 220 degrees Celsius.
2.   Combine the peppers and red onion wedges in a baking dish.
3.   Drizzle the smoked paprika with olive oil.
4.   Preheat the oven to 200°F and bake for 20-25 minutes, depending on the size of the tray.
5.   Combine the cherry tomatoes and spring on a small plate.
6.   Combine the lime zest, natural yoghurt, and lime juice in a small bowl.
7.   Heat a wide-bottomed pan with a drizzle of olive oil over medium heat.
1.   Once the pan is hot, add the drained black beans, tomato paste, and chipotle paste.
8.   After adding the vegetable stock, cook for 5-6 minutes.
9.   Top with a dollop of lime yoghurt.

Calabrian Bean & Veggie Bowls

❖ **Time to cook: 35 minutes**
❖ **Size of serving: 2**

Ingredients:

- 2 teaspoons olive oil
- seasoned with salt & pepper
- 2 tbsp. white sesame seeds
- Chilli pepper beans, 5.3 oz.
- a single lime
- 1/2 ounces fresh basil
- Parsnip, 6 oz.
- Roasted red peppers, 4 oz.
- 3 cloves garlic
- Broccoli, 6 oz.
- 1 pound cashews
- a quarter cup farro

Method:

1. Preheat the oven to 375 degrees F.
2. Combine farro and a sprinkle of salt in a small pot.
3. Bring to a boil, then reduce to medium heat and cook for 18 to 20 minutes, or until the farro is tender.
4. Toss broccoli with olive oil and salt and pepper to taste.
5. Bake for 1/2 to 15 minutes, or until tender and browned in places.
6. In a blender, add all of the ingredients for the basil cashew sauce and blend until smooth.

7.   Cook, stirring occasionally, for three to five minutes, or until the cooked farro grains are glossy and toasted.

8.   Season with salt and pepper to taste.

9.   Divide the toasted farro into large dishes.

Banh MI Bowls with Vegetables

❖   **Time to cook: 40 minutes**
❖   **4 servings**

Ingredients:

- 1/2 cup roasted peanuts
- 1/2 cup coriander
- ½ cup mayonnaise
- 2 tbsp Sirach sauce
- 1 tbsp sesame seed oil
- 1/4 cup water 1 teaspoon salt
- 1/4 cup granulated sugar
- six radishes
- a 1/2 cup risotto vinegar
- 1 cup cucumber
- two carrots
- 1 quart of water
- 1/4 cup quinoa
- 1/2 cup brown rice
- three quarts of water

Method:

1.   Half-fill a bowl with cooked quinoa.
2.   Combine the carrots, cucumber, and radishes in a mixing basin.
3.   Bring the vinegar, sesame oil, sugar, water, and salt to a boil in a small saucepan.
4.   Pour the mixture over the vegetables in the mixing basin.
5.   Set aside for 20 minutes before draining.
6.   While the vegetables are pickling, combine the mayonnaise and Sirach sauce in a small bowl.

Taco Spiced Spanish Rice Bowl

❖   **Time to cook: 25 minutes**
❖   **1 serving size**

Ingredients:

- Salt
- flour made from potatoes
- Juice of lemon
- Spices
- Garlic
- Parsley
- tomatoes, crushed
- Raisins
- Almonds in Olive Oil
- Olives from Kalamata
- Water Buckwheat
- Rice (brown)
- Feta
- Red bell peppers
- Chickpeas
- Yellow bell peppers
- Kale Onion

Method

1.   Combine one teaspoon neutral oil and one tablespoon water in a nonstick saucepan over medium heat.
2.   Cook, covered, for 10 to 15 minutes, or until the internal temperature reaches 165° F.

Conclusion

Fresh grains, meats, vegetables, and olives are staples of Mediterranean cuisine. Mediterranean meals are popular among people all over the world due to the numerous nutritional benefits they provide. The Mediterranean diet is heart-healthy because it supports fresh, low-fat, lipid-free meals. This means that you should try this recipe if you're attempting to reduce weight or just don't like eating bad foods.

While this diet does contain some animal protein, it is in small amounts and is low in fat, both of which are beneficial to your health.

All across the world, Mediterranean food is recognised for its delectable flavours and health benefits. This diet has the advantage of allowing you to consume nutritious, entire foods. You don't have to be concerned about your diet because it consists primarily of fruits, nuts, and veggies. Prepare side dishes using Mediterranean bowls cuisine to make healthy dinners for your family.